Getting Ready for Kindergarten

Angèle Sancho Passe

Getting Ready for Kindergarten

Starting kindergarten is an important, exciting, and maybe even scary step for your child—and possibly for you. Here are some ideas you can use to help your child be ready.

What Does Getting Ready for Kindergarten Mean?

Everybody has to get ready for kindergarten—children, parents, and schools alike. But what does getting ready for kindergarten mean?

Schools

For schools, getting ready means welcoming children and families. Schools invite children and their families to open houses and other welcoming events before the school year starts so they can meet the staff, tour the building, and learn the rules. For schools, getting ready also means listening to families, understanding their needs, and being sensitive to their different cultures and languages.

Parents

For parents, getting ready means preparing their children at home. Common activities help. When you talk, your child learns to exchange ideas. When you read a book, your child learns to use new words. When you write a letter, your child learns that print has meaning. When you play a board game, your child learns to take turns. And when you discuss her feelings about going to kindergarten and reassure her, your child learns to cope with new challenges.

If your child attends a preschool program, getting ready also means partnering with the caregiver. Work with the caregiver to monitor your child's growth and learning. Encourage the caregiver to read and talk to your child about the transition to kindergarten. If your child will stop seeing the caregiver once kindergarten begins, then help your child say good-bye when the time comes.

Children

For children, getting ready for kindergarten means developing the skills and behaviors necessary to do well in school. These skills and behaviors fall into five main categories:

- physical development
- social-emotional development
- language and literacy development
- cognitive development
- approaches to learning

It's important to understand these categories because educators will refer to them. Here's what they mean.

Physical development. Physical development refers to how children grow physically as well as how they use their bodies, arms, and legs to make large movements (gross-motor skills) and their fingers and hands to make small movements (fine-motor skills). To be ready for kindergarten, children need to be able use their big muscles to run and jump and their small muscles to hold a pencil and write. They need to eat and sleep well and grow healthfully.

Social-emotional development. Social-emotional development refers to how children learn about feelings. Social-emotional skills help children feel good about themselves as well as help them understand the feelings of other people. To be ready for kindergarten, children need to be able to get along with others because school is a group experience.

Language and literacy development. Language and literacy development refers to how children learn to listen, speak, read, and write. Children don't need to know how to read to be ready for kindergarten, but they should be ready to learn to read. They need to be able to listen, talk, have conversations, and ask questions. They should know about books, letters, and sounds. If children have these skills in their first language, then they will quickly learn them in a second language.

Cognitive development. Cognitive development refers to how children learn to think, make decisions, and solve problems. Children use their cognitive skills when they build a tower of blocks, play a simple board game, or finish a preschool puzzle. To be ready for kindergarten, children should know about shapes, sizes, and counting and have the ability to solve problems.

Approaches to learning. Approaches to learning refers to how children become curious about learning new things as well as how they think about what they've learned. To be ready for kindergarten, children need to develop helpful learning attitudes, like curiosity and imagination. And because learning can be hard, they should develop persistence to stick with it.

What Are Early Literacy Skills?

Children typically learn to read between kindergarten and third grade. Before kindergarten, educators focus on children's early literacy skills—skills that prepare children to learn to read, which are the foundation for school success. Research has identified the five most important early literacy skills children need:

- vocabulary
- conversation
- phonological awareness
- knowledge of the alphabet
- knowledge of books and print

You can teach these skills to your child at home. If your child attends a preschool program, caregivers there should teach your child these early literacy skills, too.

Vocabulary

To be a good reader, a child has to understand many of the words in a text and, in order to make sense of what he is reading, be able to figure out the words he doesn't already know. Here are a few ways you can help your child improve her vocabulary skills:

- Talk to your child about the things you see and do at home—when you cook, repair the faucet, or weed the garden.
- Talk to your child about what you see and do in the community—when you go to the auto shop, the dentist, or the park.
- Read books to your child, fictional stories as well as nonfiction books about animals, machines, and the natural world.
- Spend time with your child playing counting games, making charts of favorite foods, talking about nature, or sorting the laundry by color because math and science skills also rely on language.

Each of the examples provided above has special vocabulary that will enrich your child's knowledge.

Conversation

Conversation skills are also called *oral language skills*. Oral language skill is the ability to express oneself and to exchange ideas with other people. When children have a lot of practice talking, explaining, and asking questions, they become confident in their thinking and are more comfortable interacting with others at school. Here are a few ways you can help your child develop oral language skills:

- Talk with your child using vocabulary from the books you're reading with him.
- Strive for five! When you strive for five, you and your child talk and respond on the same topic for five turns. You may simply be asking questions of each other, or making comments based on each other's ideas. Here is an example.

1. **Mother:** What did you do at preschool today?
   Child: We played.
2. **Mother:** Did you play with blocks or at the sand table?
   Child: With blocks. I made a castle, a *big* castle.
3. **Mother:** You are proud of your castle!
   Child: Yeah! Tim and I, we made a big and biggest castle!
4. **Mother:** It sounds like a very fantastic castle!
   Child: Yes! It had windows and a door so the horses can get in, and Ms. B said we can work on it tomorrow, too.
5. **Mother:** What will you and Tim do tomorrow?
   Child: We are going to put on more towers, one for the king and one for the queen.

The mother helps the child elaborate, and the child uses more words and has to do more thinking as he recalls what he did today and plans what he will do tomorrow.

- Respond to your child when she initiates a conversation.

Phonological Awareness

Phonological awareness is the knowledge that there are different sounds in our world. It is also the awareness that words have sounds at their beginnings (alliteration) and at their endings (rhyming), and that words are made up of different-sounding syllables. Here are a few ways to teach your child phonological awareness:

Listen. Listen to the different sounds being made in your house—by the refrigerator, the clock, or the running faucet. At a family gathering, listen to how Grandpa and Grandma sound differently.

Rhyme. Sing songs and nursery rhymes. Point out how they rhyme. For example, in "Jack and Jill went up the hill," *Jill* and *hill* rhyme. They sound the same at their ends: *ill* and *ill*.

Alliterate. Play games with the beginning sounds of words. Come up with words that sound the same at their beginnings: *bananas, bagels,* and *breakfast,* for instance.

Play with word sounds. Change the beginning sound of your child's name: *Katie* can become *batie, datie, gatie, natie.* You'll end up making silly nonsense words together that make you laugh.

Knowledge of the Alphabet

Knowledge of the alphabet is an important tool for learning to read. The letters in the alphabet are the basis for writing because a string of letters makes a word, and the order of the letters in a word alerts us to the meaning of the word, as in *rat* and *tar.* Research tells us that if children know about fourteen of the twenty-six letters in the English alphabet at the beginning of kindergarten, they will have an easier time learning all the letters by the end of the year. Here are a few ways to teach your child the alphabet:

- Talk about the letters in your child's first and last names. Continue by discussing the letters in the names of others in your family.
- Look for letters on license plates, on store signs, in grocery store ads, and on cereal boxes. Find the letters the child already knows, and then add new ones.

Knowledge of Books and Print

Knowledge of books and print simply means understanding that books tell stories and share information. It shows children that the written word has meaning. Here are a few ways to teach your child about books and print:

- Read books to your child and talk about what you read.
- Talk about the authors and the illustrators of books you read.
- Make your own book about anything using pictures and your own words.
- Encourage your child to scribble and to write words and numbers. Children begin to write by scribbling, which develops their finger muscles. As they see adults modeling writing, they become interested in forming letters themselves. They love to write their own names.

What Does a "Ready" Child Look Like?

Children are ready for kindergarten when . . .

- ❑ They have the language to say what they think, want, feel, and need.
- ❑ They get along with children and adults.
- ❑ They understand their own feelings and the feelings of others.
- ❑ They have early literacy knowledge of vocabulary, conversation, and phonological awareness, knowledge of the alphabet, and knowledge of books and print.
- ❑ They use scribbling, writing, and drawing to represent and interpret ideas.
- ❑ They see themselves as learners and approach learning with curiosity and interest.
- ❑ They use their imagination to play and create ideas and objects.
- ❑ They are well nourished, well rested, clean, and healthy.
- ❑ They take care of their physical needs (toileting and dressing).
- ❑ They use school tools such as puzzles, scissors, computers, pencils, and markers.
- ❑ They move their bodies, legs, and arms with coordination.
- ❑ They transition between activities with ease.
- ❑ They persist at several tasks throughout the day.
- ❑ They function well in groups, sharing ideas, toys, materials, and space.
- ❑ They follow two- and three-step directions.
- ❑ They sit and participate in circle time and small groups.
- ❑ They understand they are going to a new school called *kindergarten*.

Think about how your child is doing with the items in this list. Support your child's progress at home, and work with the caregiver to support your child's progress away from home.

What Does a "Ready" Parent Look Like?

Parents are ready for kindergarten when . . .

- ❑ They provide opportunities at home for their child to talk, read, and write.
- ❑ They follow the procedures for registration, school choice, and preschool screening recommended by their school district.
- ❑ They choose a school that fits their family's needs.
- ❑ They attend informational events and workshops sponsored by the school or the school district before registration.
- ❑ They complete the kindergarten registration process in a timely manner.
- ❑ They follow through on referrals from the preschool staff to other agencies, such as special education assessment or social services.
- ❑ They visit schools.
- ❑ They meet the school's kindergarten teacher and principal after they are assigned to a school.
- ❑ They attend school orientations and events after their child is registered.
- ❑ They talk with their child about kindergarten.
- ❑ They prepare their child for the transition to kindergarten by talking about how her daily routine might change.
- ❑ They begin to develop a plan for being involved in their child's elementary school education.

A Parent's To-Do List

Parents of children entering kindergarten need to take charge of getting their child started in kindergarten. Here are the steps to follow:

Visit schools. Think about which schools in your area you might want your child to attend, and then visit those schools. Call and make an appointment before you go. During the visit, try to imagine your child as a student there and yourself as the parent of an enrolled student. It will help you decide if the school is a good match for your family.

Prepare documents for registration. Whether it's a public or a private school, registration procedures are similar. You will need to provide a copy of your child's birth certificate and a record of up-to-date immunizations from your health care provider.

Register. Some school districts have information sessions in the winter. It's important to attend them in order to learn about the school and the school district. Registration usually happens in the spring. Contact the school district or the school itself to find out dates and deadlines.

Ease the transition. Children adapt to kindergarten more easily when they have advance preparation. Talking about kindergarten helps children anticipate what it will be like, and it gives children the opportunity to ask questions and clear up misconceptions. Ease the transition by talking to your child about

- what he'll learn in kindergarten
- who else will be there—the other children, the teachers, and the principal
- what he'll do during the school day—some of the activities will be very similar to preschool, like sitting on the rug at circle time, while others will be new, like going to a noisy cafeteria for lunch
- how he'll get to and from school—will he walk, take a school bus, or get dropped off

- where he'll be before and after school—at home, in child care, or at Grandma's

Doing the following activities with your child can also help ease the transition.

- Read lots of books and talk about them.
- Have lots of conversations about everyday events.
- Tell stories to your child and listen to your child's stories.
- Sing songs and nursery rhymes.
- Count and play counting games.
- Have paper and pencil handy for drawing and scribbling.
- Color pictures and talk about them.
- Practice writing your child's name.
- Practice finding the letters of the alphabet on common items around the house.
- Play preschool board games.
- Play fantasy games—pretend to be a firefighter putting out fires, a veterinarian caring for a stuffed animal, or a bunny rabbit hopping in the forest.
- Visit the new school your child will attend.
- Meet the kindergarten teacher and the principal.
- Play on the school playground.
- Talk about your child's feelings about the new school.

Your child is ready for kindergarten when she's healthy, gets along with other children and adults, and has good early literacy skills. Support her during the transition to kindergarten so she will feel secure. Remember that you're helping your child get ready for kindergarten, and enjoy this special time together.

This is a family companion to *Is Everybody Ready for Kindergarten? A Tool Kit for Preparing Children and Families* by Angèle Sancho Passe. Angèle is a consultant and writer in early childhood education. She has taught at the University of Minnesota. She works with schools and early childhood providers to facilitate the transition to kindergarten.

Published by Redleaf Press
10 Yorkton Court
St. Paul, MN 55117
www.redleafpress.org

Cover design by Jim Handrigan
Cover photograph © Fancy Photography/Veer
Printed in the United States of America

ISBN 978-1-60554-110-5

Redleaf Press®
www.redleafpress.org
800-423-8309